NAME	DESCRIPTION	ESTABLISHED
ACADIA	Covering most of Mount Desert Island and other coastal islands, Acadia features the tallest mountain on the Atlantic coast of the United States, granite peaks, ocean shoreline, woodlands, and lakes,	FEBRUARY 26, 1919
ARCHES	Millions of years of erosion have created these structures located in a desert climate where the arid ground has life-sustaining biological soil crusts and potholes that serve as natural water-collecting basins.	NOVEMBER 12, 1971
BADLANDS	The Badlands are a collection of buttes, pinnacles, spires, and mixed-grass prairies. The White River Badlands contain the largest assemblage of known late Eocene and Oligocene mammal fossils.	NOVEMBER 10, 1978
BIG BEND	Named for the prominent bend in the Rio Grande along the U.S.–Mexico border, this park encompasses a large and remote part of the Chihuahuan Desert.	JUNE 12, 1944
BISCAYNE	Located in Biscayne Bay, this park at the north end of the Florida Keys has four interrelated marine ecosystems: mangrove forest, the Bay, the Keys, and coral reefs.	JUNE 28, 1980
BLACK CANYON OF THE GUNNISON	The park protects a quarter of the Gunnison River, which slices sheer canyon walls from dark Precambrian-era rock. The canyon features some of the steepest cliffs and oldest rock in North America.	OCTOBER 21, 1999
BRYCE CANYON	Bryce Canyon is a geological amphitheater on the Paunsaugunt Plateau with hundreds of tall, multicolored sandstone hoodoos formed by erosion. The region was originally settled by Native Americans and later by Mormon pioneers.	FEBRUARY 25, 1928
CANYONL-ANDS	This landscape was eroded into a maze of canyons, buttes, and mesas by the combined efforts of the Colorado River, Green River, and their tributaries, which divide the park into three districts.	SEPTEMBER 12, 1964
CAPITOL REEF	The park's Waterpocket Fold is a 100-mile monocline that exhibits the earth's diverse geologic layers. Other natural features include monoliths, cliffs, and sandstone domes shaped like the United States Capitol.	DECEMBER 18, 1971
CARLSBAD CAVERNS	Carlsbad Caverns has 117 caves, the longest of which is over 120 miles long. The Big Room is almost 4,000 feet long, and the caves are home to over 400,000 Mexican free-tailed bats and sixteen other species.	MAY 14, 1930

NAME	DESCRIPTION	ESTABLISHED
CHANNEL ISLANDS	Five of the eight Channel Islands are protected, with half of the park's area underwater. The islands have a unique Mediterranean ecosystem originally settled by the Chumash people.	MARCH 5, 1980
CONGAREE	On the Congaree River, this park is the largest portion of old-growth floodplain forest left in North America. Some of the trees are the tallest in the eastern United States.	NOVEMBER 10, 2003
CRATER LAKE	Crater Lake lies in the caldera of an ancient volcano called Mount Mazama that collapsed 7,700 years ago. The lake is the deepest in the United States and is noted for its vivid blue color and water clarity.	MAY 22, 1902
CUYAHOGA VALLEY	This park along the Cuyahoga River has waterfalls, hills, trails, and exhibits on early rural living. The Ohio and Erie Canal Towpath Trail follows the Ohio and Erie Canal, where mules towed canal boats.	OCTOBER 11, 2000
DEATH VALLEY	Death Valley is the hottest, lowest, and driest place in the United States, with daytime temperatures that have exceeded 130 °F (54 °C). The park protects Badwater Basin and its vast salt flats located at the lowest elevation in North America, −282 ft (−86 m).	OCTOBER 31, 1994
DENALI	Centered on Denali, the tallest and highest prominence mountain in North America, Denali is serviced by a single road leading to Wonder Lake. Denali and other peaks of the Alaska Range are covered with long glaciers and boreal forest.	FEBRUARY 26, 1917
DRY TORTUGAS	The islands of the Dry Tortugas, at the westernmost end of the Florida Keys, are the site of Fort Jefferson, a Civil War-era fort that is the largest masonry structure in the Western Hemisphere.	OCTOBER 26, 1992
EVERGLADES	The Everglades are the largest tropical wilderness in the United States. This mangrove and tropical rainforest ecosystem and marine estuary is home to 36 protected species, including the Florida panther, American crocodile, and West Indian manatee.	MAY 30, 1934
GATES OF THE ARCTIC	The country's northernmost park protects an expanse of pure wilderness in Alaska's Brooks Range and has no park facilities. The land is home to Alaska Natives .	DECEMBER 2, 1980
GATEWAY ARCH	The Gateway Arch is a 630-foot catenary arch built to commemorate the Lewis and Clark Expedition, initiated by Thomas Jefferson, and the subsequent westward expansion of the country.	FEBRUARY 22, 2018

NAME	DESCRIPTION	ESTABLISHED
GLACIER BAY	this park includes 26 glaciers and 130 named lakes surrounded by Rocky Mountain peaks. There are historic landmark road called the Going-to-the-Sun Road in this region of rapidly receding glaciers.	DECEMBER 2, 1980
GLACIER	Glacier Bay contains tidewater glaciers, mountains, fjords, and a temperate rainforest, and is home to large populations of grizzly bears, mountain goats, whales, seals, and eagles.	MAY 11, 1910
GRAND CANYON	The Grand Canyon, carved by the mighty Colorado River, is 277 miles long, up to 1 mile deep, and up to 15 miles wide. Millions of years of erosion have exposed the multicolored layers of the Colorado Plateau in mesas and canyon walls.	FEBRUARY 26, 1919
GRAND TETON	Grand Teton is the tallest mountain in the Teton Range. The park's historic Jackson Hole and reflective piedmont lakes teem with endemic wildlife, with a backdrop of craggy mountains that rise abruptly from the sage-covered valley.	FEBRUARY 26, 1929
GREAT BASIN	Based around Nevada's second tallest mountain, Wheeler Peak, Great Basin National Park contains 5,000-year-old bristlecone pines, a rock glacier, and the limestone Lehman Caves.	OCTOBER 27, 1986
GREAT SAND DUNES	The tallest sand dunes in North America, up to 750 feet (230 m) tall, were formed by deposits of the ancient Rio Grande in the San Luis Valley. Abutting a variety of grasslands, shrublands, and wetlands.	SEPTEMBER 13, 2004
GREAT SMOKY MOUNTAINS	The Great Smoky Mountains, part of the Appalachian Mountains, span a wide range of elevations, making them home to over 400 vertebrate species, 100 tree species, and 5000 plant species.	JUNE 15, 1934
GUADALUPE MOUNTAINS	This park contains Guadalupe Peak, the highest point in Texas, as well as the scenic McKittrick Canyon filled with bigtooth maples, a corner of the arid Chihuahuan Desert, and a fossilized coral reef.	OCTOBER 15, 1966
HALEAKALA	The Haleakalā volcano on Maui features a very large crater with numerous cinder cones, Hosmer's Grove of alien trees, the Kipahulu section's scenic pools of freshwater fish, and the native Hawaiian goose.	JULY 1, 1961
HAWAI'I VOLCANOES	This park on the Big Island protects the Kīlauea and Mauna Loa volcanoes, two of the world's most active geological features. Diverse ecosystems range from tropical forests at sea level to barren lava beds.	AUGUST 1, 1916

NAME	DESCRIPTION	ESTABLISHED
HOT SPRINGS	Hot Springs was established as a federal reserve by Congress on April 20, 1832—the oldest area managed by the National Park Service. Congress redesignated Hot Springs as a national park on March 4, 1921.	MARCH 4, 1921
INDIANA DUNES	Previously designated a national lakeshore, the dunes run for nearly 25 miles along the southern shore of Lake Michigan. The sandy beach adjoins a grassy prairie, and wetlands home to over 2,000 species.	FEBRUARY 15, 2019
ISLE ROYALE	The largest island in Lake Superior is a place of isolation and wilderness. Along with its many shipwrecks, waterways, and hiking trails, the park also includes over 400 smaller islands within 4.5 miles (7.2 km) of its shores.	APRIL 3, 1940
JOSHUA TREE	Covering large areas of the Colorado and Mojave Deserts and the Little San Bernardino Mountains, this desert landscape is populated by vast stands of Joshua trees.	OCTOBER 31, 1994
KATMAI	his park on the Alaska Peninsula protects the Valley of Ten Thousand Smokes, an ash flow formed by the 1912 eruption of Novarupta, as well as Mount Katmai. Over 2,000 grizzly bears come here each year to catch spawning salmon.	DECEMBER 2, 1980
KENAI FJORDS	Near Seward on the Kenai Peninsula, this park protects the Harding Icefield and at least 38 glaciers and fjords stemming from it. The only area accessible to the public by road is Exit Glacier.	DECEMBER 2, 1980
KINGS CANYON	Home to several giant sequoia groves and the General Grant Tree, the world's second largest measured tree, this park also features part of the Kings River, sculptor of the dramatic granite canyon that is its namesake.	MARCH 4, 1940
KOBUK VALLEY	Kobuk Valley protects 61 miles of the Kobuk River and three regions of sand dunes. Created by glaciers, the Great Kobuk, Little Kobuk, and Hunt River Sand Dunes can reach 100 feet high and 100 °F (38 °C), and they are the largest dunes in the Arctic.	DECEMBER 2, 1980
LAKE CLARK	The region around Lake Clark features four active volcanoes, including Mount Redoubt, as well as an abundance of rivers, glaciers, and waterfalls.	DECEMBER 2, 1980
LASSEN VOLCANIC	Lassen Peak, the largest lava dome volcano in the world, is joined by all three other types of volcanoes in this park: shield, cinder cone, and composite. Though Lassen itself last erupted in 1915, most of the rest of the park is continuously active.	AUGUST 9, 1916

NAME	DESCRIPTION	ESTABLISHED
MAMMOTH CAVE	With more than 400 miles of passageways explored, Mammoth Cave is the world's longest known cave system. Subterranean wildlife includes eight bat species, Northern cavefish, and cave salamanders.	JULY 1, 1941
MESA VERDE	This area constitutes over 4,000 archaeological sites of the Ancestral Puebloan people, who lived here and elsewhere in the Four Corners region for at least 700 years.	JUNE 29, 1906
MOUNT RAINIER	Mount Rainier, an active stratovolcano, is the most prominent peak in the Cascades and is covered by 26 named glaciers including Carbon Glacier and Emmons Glacier, the largest in the contiguous United States.	MARCH 2, 1899
NP OF AMERICAN SAMOA	The southernmost national park is on three Samoan islands and protects coral reefs, rainforests, volcanic mountains, and white beaches. The area is also home to flying foxes, brown boobies, sea turtles, and 900 species of fish.	OCTOBER 31, 1988
NORTH CASCADES	This complex includes two geographically distinct units of the national park, as well as Ross Lake and Lake Chelan National Recreation Areas. The highly glaciated mountains are spectacular examples of Cascade geology.	OCTOBER 2, 1968
OLYMPIC	Situated on the Olympic Peninsula, this park includes a wide range of ecosystems from Pacific shoreline to temperate rainforests to the alpine slopes of the Olympic Mountains, the tallest of which is Mount Olympus.	JUNE 29, 1938
PETRIFIED FOREST	This portion of the Chinle Formation has a large concentration of 225-million-year-old petrified wood. The surrounding Painted Desert features eroded cliffs of red-hued volcanic rock called bentonite.	DECEMBER 9, 1962
PINNACLES	Named for the eroded leftovers of a portion of an extinct volcano, the park's massive black and gold monoliths of andesite and rhyolite are a popular destination for rock climbers.	JANUARY 10, 2013
REDWOOD	This park and the co-managed state parks protect almost half of all remaining coastal redwoods, the tallest trees on earth. There are three large river systems in this very seismically active area, and 37 miles of protected coastline reveal tide pools.	OCTOBER 2, 1968
ROCKY MOUNTAIN	Bisected north to south by the Continental Divide, this portion of the Rockies has ecosystems varying from over 150 riparian lakes to montane and subalpine forests to treeless alpine tundra.	JANUARY 26, 1915

NAME	DESCRIPTION	ESTABLISHED
SAGUARO	Split into the separate Rincon Mountain and Tucson Mountain districts, this park is evidence that the dry Sonoran Desert is still home to a great variety of life spanning six biotic communities.	OCTOBER 14, 1994
SEQUOIA	This park protects the Giant Forest, which boasts some of the world's largest trees, the General Sherman being the largest measured tree in the park.	SEPTEMBER 25, 1890
SHENAND-OAH	Shenandoah's Blue Ridge Mountains are covered by hardwood forests that teem with a wide variety of wildlife. The Skyline Drive and Appalachian Trail run the entire length of this narrow park.	DECEMBER 26, 1935
THEODORE ROOSEVEL	This region that enticed and influenced President Theodore Roosevelt consists of a park of three units in the northern badlands. Besides Roosevelt's historic cabin, there are numerous scenic drives and backcountry hiking opportunities.	NOVEMBER 10, 1978
VIRGIN ISLANDS	This island park on Saint John preserves Taíno archaeological sites and the ruins of sugar plantations from Columbus's time, as well as all the natural environs.	AUGUST 2, 1956
VOYAGEURS	This park protecting four lakes near the Canada–US border is a site for canoeing, kayaking, and fishing. The park also preserves a history populated by Ojibwe Native Americans.	APRIL 8, 1975
WHITE SANDS	Located in the mountain-ringed Tularosa Basin, White Sands consists of the southern part of a 275-square-mile (710 km2) field of white sand dunes composed of gypsum crystals—the world's largest gypsum dunefield.	DECEMBER 20, 2019
WIND CAVE	Wind Cave is distinctive for its calcite fin formations called boxwork, a unique formation rarely found elsewhere, and needle-like growths called frostwork. The cave is one of the longest and most complex caves in the world.	JANUARY 9, 1903
WRANGELL-ST. ELIAS	An over 8 million acres (32,375 km2) plot of mountainous country—the largest national park in the system—protects the convergence of the Alaska, Chugach, and Wrangell-Saint Elias Ranges.	DECEMBER 2, 1980
YELLOWS-TONE	Situated on the Yellowstone Caldera, the park has an expansive network of geothermal areas including boiling mud pots, vividly colored hot springs such as Grand Prismatic Spring, and regularly erupting geysers, the best-known being Old Faithful.	MARCH 1, 1872

NAME	DESCRIPTION	ESTABLISHED
YOSEMITE	Yosemite features sheer granite cliffs, exceptionally tall waterfalls, and old-growth forests at a unique intersection of geology and hydrology. Half Dome and El Capitan rise from the park's centerpiece	OCTOBER 1, 1890
ZION	Located at the junction of the Colorado Plateau, Great Basin, and Mojave Desert, this park contains sandstone features such as mesas, rock towers, and canyons, including the Virgin River Narrows.	NOVEMBER 19, 1919

NATIONAL PARKS
← US ≪
TRACKING LOG

ALASKA

U.S NATIONAL PARK	ORDER	VISITED
ACADIA		
GATES OF THE ARCTIC		
GLACIER BAY		
KATMAI		
KENAI FJORDS		
KOBUK VALLEY		
LAKE CLARK		
WRANGELL-ST. ELIAS		

AMERICAN SAMOA

U.S NATIONAL PARK	ORDER	VISITED
NATIONAL PARK OF AMERICAN SAMOA		

ARIZONA

U.S NATIONAL PARK	ORDER	VISITED
GRAND CANYON		
PETRIFIED FOREST		
SAGUARO		

ARKANSAS

U.S NATIONAL PARK	ORDER	VISITED
HOT SPRINGS		

CALIFORNIA

U.S NATIONAL PARK	ORDER	VISITED
CHANNEL ISLANDS		
DEATH VALLEY		
JOSHUA TREE		
KINGS CANYON		
LASSEN VOLCANIC		
PINNACLES		
REDWOOD		
SEQUOIA		
YOSEMITE		

COLORADO

U.S NATIONAL PARK	ORDER	VISITED
BLACK CANYON OF THE GUNNISON		
GREAT SAND DUNES		
MESA VERDE		
ROCKY MOUNTAIN		

FLORIDA

U.S NATIONAL PARK	ORDER	VISITED
BISCAYNE NATIONAL		
DRY TORTUGAS		
EVERGLADES		

HAWAII

U.S NATIONAL PARK	ORDER	VISITED
HALEAKALA		
HAWAI'I VOLCANOES		

IDAHO

U.S NATIONAL PARK	ORDER	VISITED
YELLOWSTONE		

KENTUCKY

U.S NATIONAL PARK	ORDER	VISITED
MAMMOTH CAVE		

INDIANA

U.S NATIONAL PARK	ORDER	VISITED
INDIANA DUNES		

MAINE

U.S NATIONAL PARK	ORDER	VISITED
ACADIA		

MICHIGAN

U.S NATIONAL PARK	ORDER	VISITED
ISLE ROYALE		

MINNESOTA

U.S NATIONAL PARK	ORDER	VISITED
VOYAGEURS		

MISSOURI

U.S NATIONAL PARK	ORDER	VISITED
GATEWAY ARCH		

MONTANA

U.S NATIONAL PARK	ORDER	VISITED
GLACIER		
YELLOWSTONE		✓

NEVADA

U.S NATIONAL PARK	ORDER	VISITED
DEATH VALLEY		
GREAT BASIN		

NEW MEXICO

U.S NATIONAL PARK	ORDER	VISITED
CARLSBAD CAVERNS		
WHITE SANDS		

NORTH DAKOTA

U.S NATIONAL PARK	ORDER	VISITED
THEODORE ROOSEVELT		

NORTH CAROLINA

U.S NATIONAL PARK	ORDER	VISITED
GREAT SMOKY MOUNTAINS		

OHIO

U.S NATIONAL PARK	ORDER	VISITED
CUYAHOGA VALLEY		

OREGON

U.S NATIONAL PARK	ORDER	VISITED
CRATER LAKE		

SOUTH CAROLINA

U.S NATIONAL PARK	ORDER	VISITED
CONGAREE		

SOUTH DAKOTA

U.S NATIONAL PARK	ORDER	VISITED
BADLANDS		
WIND CAVE		

TENNESSEE

U.S NATIONAL PARK	ORDER	VISITED
GREAT SMOKY MOUNTAINS		

TEXAS

U.S NATIONAL PARK	ORDER	VISITED
BIG BEND		
GUADALUPE MOUNTAINS		

UTAH

U.S NATIONAL PARK	ORDER	VISITED
ARCHES		
BRYCE CANYON		
CANYONLANDS		
CAPITOL REEF		
ZION		

VIRGIN ISLANDS

U.S NATIONAL PARK	ORDER	VISITED
VIRGIN ISLANDS		

VIRGINIA

U.S NATIONAL PARK	ORDER	VISITED
SHENANDOAH		

WASHINGTON

U.S NATIONAL PARK	ORDER	VISITED
MOUNT RAINIER		
NORTH CASCADES		
OLYMPIC		

WYOMING

U.S NATIONAL PARK	ORDER	VISITED
GRAND TETON		
YELLOWSTONE		

U.S. NATIONAL PARKS MAP

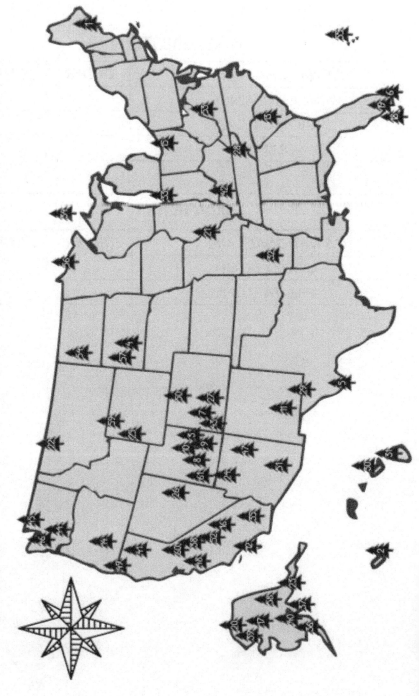

NATIONAL PARKS CHECKLIST

- ☐ 1. ACADIA (ME)
- ☐ 2. AMERICAN SAMOA
- ☐ 3. ARCHES (UT)
- ☐ 4. BADLANDS (SD)
- ☐ 5. BIG BEND (TX)
- ☐ 6. BISCAYNE (FL)
- ☐ 7. BLACK CANYON (CO)
- ☐ 8. BRYCE CANYON (UT)
- ☐ 9. CANYONLANDS (UT)
- ☐ 10. CAPITOL REEF (UT)
- ☐ 11. CARLSBAD CAVERNS (NM)
- ☐ 12. CHANNEL ISLANDS (CA)
- ☐ 13. CONGAREE (SC)
- ☐ 14. CRATER LAKE (OR)
- ☐ 15. CUYAHOGA (OH)
- ☐ 16. DEATH VALLEY (CA)
- ☐ 17. DENALI (AK)
- ☐ 18. DRY TORTUGAS (FL)
- ☐ 19. EVERGLADES (FL)
- ☐ 20. GATES OF THE ARCTIC (AK)
- ☐ 21. GATEWAY ARCH (MO)
- ☐ 22. GLACIER (MT)
- ☐ 23. GLACIER BAY (AK)
- ☐ 24. GRAND CANYON (AZ)
- ☐ 25. GRAND TETON (WY)
- ☐ 26. GREAT BASIN (NV)
- ☐ 27. GREAT SAND DUNES (CO)
- ☐ 28. GREAT SMOKY MOUNTAINS (TN)
- ☐ 29. GUADALUPE MOUNTAINS (TX)
- ☐ 30. HALEAKALA (HI)
- ☐ 31. HAWAII VOLCANOES (HI)
- ☐ 32. HOT SPRINGS (AR)
- ☐ 33. INDIANA DUNES (IN)
- ☐ 34. ISLE ROYALE (MI)
- ☐ 35. JOSHUA TREE (CA)
- ☐ 36. KATMAI (AK)
- ☐ 37. KENAI FJORDS (AK)
- ☐ 38. KINGS CANYON (CA)
- ☐ 39. KOBUK VALLEY (AK)
- ☐ 40. LAKE CLARK (AK)
- ☐ 41. LASSEN VOLCANIC (CA)
- ☐ 42. MAMMOTH CAVE (KY)
- ☐ 43. MESA VERDE (CO)
- ☐ 44. MOUNT RAINIER (WA)
- ☐ 45. NORTH CASCADES (WA)
- ☐ 46. OLYMPIC (WA)
- ☐ 47. PETRIFIED FOREST (AZ)
- ☐ 48. PINNACLES (CA)
- ☐ 49. REDWOOD (CA)
- ☐ 50. ROCKY MOUNTAIN (CO)
- ☐ 51. SAGUARO (AZ)
- ☐ 52. SEQUOIA (CA)
- ☐ 53. SHENANDOAH (VA)
- ☐ 54. THEODORE ROOSEVELT (ND)
- ☐ 55. VIRGIN ISLANDS
- ☐ 56. VOYAGEURS (MN)
- ☐ 57. WIND CAVE (SD)
- ☐ 58. WRANGELL - ST. ELIAS (AK)
- ☑ 59. YELLOWSTONE (WY)
- ☐ 60. YOSEMITE (CA)
- ☐ 61. ZION (UT)

MY BUCKET LIST

N°	U.S NATIONAL PARK NAME	DATE
1		
2		
3		
4		
5		
6		
7		
8		
9		
10		
11		
12		
13		
14		
15		
16		
17		
18		
19		
20		
21		
22		
23		
24		
25		
26		
27		
28		
29		
30		
31		

MY BUCKET LIST

N°	U.S NATIONAL PARK NAME	DATE
32		
33		
34		
35		
36		
37		
38		
39		
40		
41		
42		
43		
44		
45		
46		
47		
48		
49		
50		
51		
52		
53		
54		
55		
56		
57		
58		
59		
60		
61		
62		

NATIONAL PARKS

← US ←

in Alphabetical Order

A

ACADIA NATIONAL PARK, **MAINE**

ARCHES NATIONAL PARK, **UTAH**

B

BADLANDS NATIONAL PARK, **SOUTH DAKOTA**

BIG BEND NATIONAL PARK, **TEXAS**

BISCAYNE NATIONAL PARK, **FLORIDA**

BLACK CANYON OF THE GUNNISON NATIONAL PARK, **COLORADO**

BRYCE CANYON NATIONAL PARK, **UTAH**

C

CANYONLANDS NATIONAL PARK, **UTAH**

CAPITOL REEF NATIONAL PARK, **UTAH**

CARLSBAD CAVERNS NATIONAL PARK, **NEW MEXICO**

CHANNEL ISLANDS NATIONAL PARK, **CALIFORNIA**

CONGAREE NATIONAL PARK, **SOUTH CAROLINA**

CRATER LAKE NATIONAL PARK, **OREGON**

CUYAHOGA VALLEY NATIONAL PARK, **OHIO**

D

DEATH VALLEY NATIONAL PARK, **CALIFORNIA AND NEVADA**

DENALI NATIONAL PARK, **ALASKA**

DRY TORTUGAS NATIONAL PARK, **FLORIDA**

E

EVERGLADES NATIONAL PARK, **FLORIDA**

G

GATES OF THE ARCTIC NATIONAL PARK, **ALASKA**

GATEWAY ARCH NATIONAL PARK, **MISSOURI AND ILLINOIS**

GLACIER BAY NATIONAL PARK, **ALASKA**

GLACIER NATIONAL PARK, **MONTANA**

GRAND CANYON NATIONAL PARK, **ARIZONA**

GRAND TETON NATIONAL PARK, **WYOMING**

GREAT BASIN NATIONAL PARK, **NEVADA**

GREAT SAND DUNES NATIONAL PARK, **COLORADO**

GREAT SMOKY MOUNTAINS NATIONAL PARK,
NORTH CAROLINA AND TENNESSEE

GUADALUPE MOUNTAINS NATIONAL PARK, **TEXAS**

H

HALEAKALA NATIONAL PARK, **HAWAII**

HAWAI'I VOLCANOES NATIONAL PARK, **HAWAII**

HOT SPRINGS NATIONAL PARK, **ARKANSAS**

I

INDIANA DUNES NATIONAL PARK, **INDIANA**

ISLE ROYALE NATIONAL PARK, **MICHIGAN**

J

JOSHUA TREE NATIONAL PARK, **CALIFORNIA**

K

KATMAI NATIONAL PARK, **ALASKA**

KENAI FJORDS NATIONAL PARK, **ALASKA**

KINGS CANYON NATIONAL PARK, **CALIFORNIA**

KOBUK VALLEY NATIONAL PARK, **ALASKA**

L

LAKE CLARK NATIONAL PARK, **ALASKA**

LASSEN VOLCANIC NATIONAL PARK, **CALIFORNIA**

M

MAMMOTH CAVE NATIONAL PARK, **KENTUCKY**

MESA VERDE NATIONAL PARK, **COLORADO**

MOUNT RAINIER NATIONAL PARK, **WASHINGTON**

N

NATIONAL PARK OF AMERICAN SAMOA, **AMERICAN SAMOA**

NORTH CASCADES NATIONAL PARK, **WASHINGTON**

O

OLYMPIC NATIONAL PARK, **WASHINGTON**

P

PETRIFIED FOREST NATIONAL PARK, **ARIZONA**

PINNACLES NATIONAL PARK, **CALIFORNIA**

R

REDWOOD NATIONAL PARK, **CALIFORNIA**
ROCKY MOUNTAIN NATIONAL PARK, **COLORADO**

S

SAGUARO NATIONAL PARK, **ARIZONA**
SEQUOIA NATIONAL PARK, **CALIFORNIA**
SHENANDOAH NATIONAL PARK, **VIRGINIA**

T

THEODORE ROOSEVELT NATIONAL PARK, **NORTH DAKOTA**

V

VIRGIN ISLANDS NATIONAL PARK, **VIRGIN ISLANDS**
VOYAGEURS NATIONAL PARK, **MINNESOTA**

N

WHITE SANDS NATIONAL PARK, **NEW MEXICO**
WIND CAVE NATIONAL PARK, **SOUTH DAKOTA**

WRANGELL-ST. ELIAS NATIONAL PARK, **ALASKA**

Y

YELLOWSTONE NATIONAL PARK,
IDAHO, MONTANA, AND WYOMING
YOSEMITE NATIONAL PARK, **CALIFORNIA**

Z

ZION NATIONAL PARK, **UTAH**

STORAGE

	Current state	Necessary State	Where to get/learn/buy
Equipment			
Skills			
Condition			
Knowledge			
Knowing the area i'm going to visit			

STORAGE

	Current state	Necessary State	Where to get/learn/buy
Equipment			
Skills			
Condition			
Knowledge			
Knowing the area i'm going to visit			

STORAGE

	Current state	Necessary State	Where to get/learn/buy
Equipment			
Skills			
Condition			
Knowledge			
Knowing the area i'm going to visit			

STORAGE

	Current state	Necessary State	Where to get/learn/buy
Equipment			
Skills			
Condition			
Knowledge			
Knowing the area i'm going to visit			

STORAGE

	Current state	Necessary State	Where to get/learn/buy
Equipment			
Skills			
Condition			
Knowledge			
Knowing the area i'm going to visit			

ARCADIA

Lodging

_____

FEE(S) :

WEBSITE :
www.nps.gov/acad

PHONE NUMBER :
207/288-3338

Weather

°F
(   )

MOOD : _____
_____

I AM WITH : _____

_____

_____

MY EXPECTATIONS : _____

_____

_____

WILDLIFE

SIGHTS

≫ — ATTRACTIONS I VISITED ⟶

○ Cadillac Mountain   ○ Schoodic Point   ○ _____
○ Park Loop Road   ○ Sand Beach   ○ _____
○ Jordan Pond   ○ Thunder Hole   ○ _____

VISITOR CENTER INFORMATION, NOTES, SKETCHES, etc.

My Best Moments

_____

_____

_____

— *few words about* —
—— *my visit* ——

- -

- -

- -

- -

stamp here

RATING ☆☆☆☆☆

← UTAH →≪

ARCHES

Lodging

_____

FEE(S) :

WEBSITE :
www.nps.gov/arch

PHONE NUMBER :
435/719-2299

Weather

°F
( )

MOOD : _____
_____

I AM WITH : _____
_____
_____

MY EXPECTATIONS : _____
_____
_____

WILDLIFE

SIGHTS

≫— ATTRACTIONS I VISITED —→

○ Arches Scenic Drive   ○ Fiery Furnace   ○ _____
○ Balanced Rock   ○ Landscape Arch   ○ _____
○ Delicate Arch   ○ Double Arch   ○ _____

VISITOR CENTER INFORMATION, NOTES, SKETCHES, etc.

My Best Moments

_____

_____

_____

_____ *few words about* _____
_____ *my visit* _____

----

stamp here

RATING ☆☆☆☆☆

VISIT DATE
__ / __ /20__

← SOUTH DAKOTA ←≪

PARK N°
_____

BADLANDS

Lodging

_____

FEE(S) :

WEBSITE :
www.nps.gov/badl

PHONE NUMBER :
605/433-5361

Weather

°F
( )

MOOD : _____
_____

I AM WITH : _____
_____
_____

MY EXPECTATIONS : _____
_____
_____

WILDLIFE

SIGHTS

≫—— ATTRACTIONS I VISITED ——→

○ Rent A Cabin
○ Stargaze
○ Badlands Loop Road

○ Visit the prairie
○ Walk Fossil Trail
○ Enjoy A Sioux Taco

○ ---------------
○ ---------------
○ ---------------

VISITOR CENTER INFORMATION, NOTES, SKETCHES, etc.

My Best Moments

---

few words about
my visit

---

stamp here

RATING ☆☆☆☆☆

BIG BEND

Lodging

FEE(S) :

WEBSITE :
www.nps.gov/bibe

PHONE NUMBER :
432/477-2251

Weather

°F
( )

MOOD :

I AM WITH :

MY EXPECTATIONS :

WILDLIFE

SIGHTS

≫—— **ATTRACTIONS I VISITED** ⟶

○ Santa Elena Canyon   ○ Chisos Mountains   ○ -------------

○ Lost Mine Trail   ○ El Camino Del Rio   ○ -------------

○ The Window Trail   ○ The Balanced Rock   ○ -------------

VISITOR CENTER INFORMATION, NOTES, SKETCHES, etc.

— My Best Moments —

_____

_____

_____

— *few words about* —
—— *my visit* ——

- -

- -

- -

- -

stamp here

RATING ☆☆☆☆☆

BISCAYNE

Lodging

_____

FEE(S) :

WEBSITE :
www.nps.gov/bisc

PHONE NUMBER :
305/230-1144

Weather

°F
( )

MOOD : _____
_____

I AM WITH : _____
_____
_____

MY EXPECTATIONS : _____
_____
_____

WILDLIFE

SIGHTS

≫ — ATTRACTIONS I VISITED ⟶

○ Boca Chita Key
○ Boat Tour
○ Fishing

○ Canoeing/Kayaking
○ Elliott Key
○ Stiltsville

○ _____
○ _____
○ _____

VISITOR CENTER INFORMATION, NOTES, SKETCHES, etc.

———— My Best Moments ————

—— few words about ——
—— my visit ——

stamp here

RATING ☆☆☆☆☆

VISIT DATE		PARK N°
/ /20	← COLORADO ≪	

BLACK CANYON OF THE GUNNISON

Lodging

_____

FEE(S) :	WEBSITE : www.nps.gov/blca	PHONE NUMBER : 970/641-2337, ext. 205

Weather ☀ ⛅ 🌧 ⛈ ❄	°F ( )	MOOD : _____

I AM WITH : _____	MY EXPECTATIONS : _____
_____	_____
_____	_____

WILDLIFE	SIGHTS

≫ — ATTRACTIONS I VISITED ⟶

○ Experience the Views   ○ Boat Down the River   ○ _____
○ Camping   ○ See the Skies   ○ _____
○ Fishing   ○ Visit the North Rim   ○ _____

VISITOR CENTER INFORMATION, NOTES, SKETCHES, etc.

My Best Moments

— few words about —
— my visit —

stamp here

RATING ☆☆☆☆☆

BRYCE CANYON

Lodging

FEE(S) :

WEBSITE :
www.nps.gov/brca

PHONE NUMBER :
435/834-5322

Weather

°F
( )

MOOD :

I AM WITH :

MY EXPECTATIONS :

WILDLIFE

SIGHTS

≫ — ATTRACTIONS I VISITED — →

○ Inspiration Point
○ Bryce Point
○ Sunrise Point

○ Scenic Drive
○ Yovimpa Point
○ Rainbow Point

○ --------------
○ --------------
○ --------------

VISITOR CENTER INFORMATION, NOTES, SKETCHES, etc.

My Best Moments

_____

_____

_____

— few words about —
— my visit —

----

stamp here

RATING ☆☆☆☆☆

CANYONLANDS

Lodging

_____

FEE(S) :

WEBSITE :
www.nps.gov/cany

PHONE NUMBER :
435/719-2313

Weather

°F
( )

MOOD : _____
_____

I AM WITH : _____
_____
_____

MY EXPECTATIONS : _____
_____
_____

WILDLIFE

SIGHTS

≫— ATTRACTIONS I VISITED —→

○ Grand view point
○ Mesa arch
○ Green river overlook

○ Shafer canyon
○ Buck canyon overlook
○ Upheaval dome

○ _____
○ _____
○ _____

VISITOR CENTER INFORMATION, NOTES, SKETCHES, etc.

My Best Moments

_____

_____

_____

— few words about —
— my visit —

----

stamp here

RATING ☆☆☆☆☆

CAPITOL REEF

Lodging

_____

FEE(S) :

WEBSITE :
www.nps.gov/care

PHONE NUMBER :
435/425-3791

Weather

°F
( )

MOOD : _____

I AM WITH : _____

_____

_____

MY EXPECTATIONS : _____

_____

_____

WILDLIFE

SIGHTS

≫— **ATTRACTIONS I VISITED** ⟶

○ Burr Trail
○ Cassidy Arch
○ Fruita

○ Fremont Petroglyphs
○ Cathedral Valley
○ Goosenecks Overlook

○ _____
○ _____
○ _____

VISITOR CENTER INFORMATION, NOTES, SKETCHES, etc.

My Best Moments

_____

_____

_____

— few words about —
— my visit —

----

stamp here

RATING ☆☆☆☆☆

CARLSBAD CAVERNS

Lodging

FEE(S) :

WEBSITE :
www.nps.gov/cave

PHONE NUMBER :
575/785-2232

Weather

°F
( )

MOOD : _____

I AM WITH : _____

MY EXPECTATIONS : _____

WILDLIFE

SIGHTS

≫── ATTRACTIONS I VISITED ──→

- ○ Big Room
- ○ Bat Flight Program
- ○ King's Palace

- ○ Bottomless Pit
- ○ Giant dome
- ○ Lion's tail

- ○ ---------------
- ○ ---------------
- ○ ---------------

VISITOR CENTER INFORMATION, NOTES, SKETCHES, etc.

—— My Best Moments ——

—— *few words about* —— *my visit* ——

stamp here

RATING ☆☆☆☆☆

CHANNEL ISLANDS

Lodging

_____

FEE(S) :

WEBSITE :	PHONE NUMBER :
www.nps.gov/chis	805/658-5730

Weather

°F
( )

MOOD : _____
_____

I AM WITH : _____
_____
_____

MY EXPECTATIONS : _____
_____
_____

WILDLIFE

SIGHTS

≫ — ATTRACTIONS I VISITED ⟶

- ◯ Plemont Bay
- ◯ Elizabeth Castle
- ◯ Victoria Tower
- ◯ The SandWizard
- ◯ Castle Cornet
- ◯ Le Petit Train
- ◯ ---------------
- ◯ ---------------
- ◯ ---------------

VISITOR CENTER INFORMATION, NOTES, SKETCHES, etc.

My Best Moments

_____

_____

_____

— few words about —
— my visit —

- -

- -

- -

- -

stamp here

RATING ☆☆☆☆☆

VISIT DATE	←—SOUTH CAROLINA—≪	PARK N°
__ / __ /20__		

CONGAREE

Lodging

_____

FEE(S) :

WEBSITE :
www.nps.gov/cong

PHONE NUMBER :
803/776-4396

Weather

°F
( )

MOOD : _____
_____

I AM WITH : _____
_____
_____

MY EXPECTATIONS : _____
_____
_____

WILDLIFE

SIGHTS

≫ ATTRACTIONS I VISITED ⟶

○ Hiking a Trail   ○ Ranger Led Canoe   ○ _____
○ Walk and Talk   ○ Synchronous Fireflies ○ _____
○ Canoe or Kayak   ○ Camping   ○ _____

VISITOR CENTER INFORMATION, NOTES, SKETCHES, etc.

My Best Moments

_____

_____

_____

— few words about —
——— my visit ———

- -

- -

- -

- -

stamp here

RATING ☆☆☆☆☆

← — OREGON — ≪

CRATER LAKE

Lodging

_____

FEE(S) :

WEBSITE :
www.nps.gov/crla

PHONE NUMBER :
541/594-3000

Weather

°F
( )

MOOD : _____
_____

I AM WITH : _____
_____
_____

MY EXPECTATIONS : _____
_____
_____

WILDLIFE

SIGHTS

≫ — ATTRACTIONS I VISITED ⟶

○ Drive the Rim Drive   ○ Hike Garfield Peak   ○ ----------------
○ Crater Lake Lodge   ○ Watch the Sunrise   ○ ----------------
○ Visit Wizard Island   ○ See Plaikni Falls   ○ ----------------

VISITOR CENTER INFORMATION, NOTES, SKETCHES, etc.

My Best Moments

_____

_____

_____

— *few words about* —
—— *my visit* ——

----

stamp here

RATING ☆☆☆☆☆

CUYAHOGA VALLEY

Lodging

FEE(S) :

WEBSITE :
www.nps.gov/cuva

PHONE NUMBER :
330/657-2752

Weather

°F
( )

MOOD : ____

I AM WITH : _____

MY EXPECTATIONS : _____

WILDLIFE

SIGHTS

≫— ATTRACTIONS I VISITED ⟶

○ The ledges trail   ○ Brandywine falls   ○ --------------
○ Blue hen falls   ○ Cuyahoga valley   ○ --------------
○ Canal exploration   ○ Beaver marsh   ○ --------------

VISITOR CENTER INFORMATION, NOTES, SKETCHES, etc.

My Best Moments

_____

_____

_____

— few words about —
—— my visit ——

- -

- -

- -

- -

stamp here

RATING ☆ ☆ ☆ ☆ ☆

DEATH VALLEY

Lodging

_____

FEE(S) :

WEBSITE :
www.nps.gov/deva

PHONE NUMBER :
760/786-3200

Weather

°F
( )

MOOD : _____
_____

I AM WITH : _____

MY EXPECTATIONS : _____

WILDLIFE

SIGHTS

≫——————— **ATTRACTIONS I VISITED** ———→

○ Badwater
○ Zabriskie Point
○ Dante's View

○ Artist's Drive
○ Artists Palette
○ Titus Canyon

○ _____
○ _____
○ _____

VISITOR CENTER INFORMATION, NOTES, SKETCHES, etc.

My Best Moments

_____

_____

_____

— *few words about* —
——— *my visit* ———

----

stamp here

RATING ☆☆☆☆☆

← ALASKA →

DENALI

Lodging

FEE(S) :

WEBSITE :
www,nps,gov/dena

PHONE NUMBER :
907/683-9532

Weather

°F
( )

MOOD :

I AM WITH :

MY EXPECTATIONS :

WILDLIFE

SIGHTS

≫— ATTRACTIONS I VISITED →

○ Eielson Center ○ Horseshoe Lake ○ --------------
○ Park road   ○ Savage Alpine   ○ --------------
○ Wonder lake   ○ Savage river   ○ --------------

VISITOR CENTER INFORMATION, NOTES, SKETCHES, etc.

My Best Moments

few words about
my visit

stamp here

RATING ☆☆☆☆☆

VISIT DATE	← FLORIDA ⟪	PARK N°
_ _ / _ /20_		_ _ _ _ _ _ _

DRY TORTUGAS

Lodging

_____

FEE(S) :	WEBSITE : www.nps.gov/drto	PHONE NUMBER : 305/242-7700

Weather

°F
( )

MOOD : _____
_____

I AM WITH : _ _ _ _ _ _ _ _ _ _
_ _ _ _ _ _ _ _ _ _ _ _ _ _ _
_ _ _ _ _ _ _ _ _ _ _ _ _ _ _

MY EXPECTATIONS : _ _ _ _ _ _
_ _ _ _ _ _ _ _ _ _ _ _ _ _ _
_ _ _ _ _ _ _ _ _ _ _ _ _ _ _

WILDLIFE

SIGHTS

⟫ — **ATTRACTIONS I VISITED** ⟶

- ◯ Bird watching
- ◯ Snorkeling
- ◯ Tent Camping
- ◯ Explore the Beaches
- ◯ Fort Jefferson
- ◯ Trip by catamaran
- ◯ _ _ _ _ _ _ _ _ _
- ◯ _ _ _ _ _ _ _ _ _
- ◯ _ _ _ _ _ _ _ _ _

VISITOR CENTER INFORMATION, NOTES, SKETCHES, etc.

My Best Moments

_____ few words about _____
_____ my visit _____

----

stamp here

RATING ☆☆☆☆☆

← FLORIDA ←

EVERGLADES

Lodging

FEE(S) :

WEBSITE :
www.nps.gov/ever

PHONE NUMBER :
305/242-7700

Weather

°F
( )

MOOD : ___

I AM WITH : ___

MY EXPECTATIONS : ___

WILDLIFE

SIGHTS

≫ — **ATTRACTIONS I VISITED** ⟶

- ○ Airboat Tours
- ○ Shark Valley Tram
- ○ Observation Tower
- ○ Hiking
- ○ Bicycle Tours
- ○ Canoe the Glades
- ○ ___
- ○ ___
- ○ ___

VISITOR CENTER INFORMATION, NOTES, SKETCHES, etc.

My Best Moments

_____

_____

_____

— few words about —
— my visit —

- -

- -

- -

- -

stamp here

RATING ☆☆☆☆☆

GATES OF THE ARCTIC
Lodging

FEE(S) :

WEBSITE :
www.nps.gov/gaar

PHONE NUMBER :
907/692-5494

Weather

°F
( )

MOOD :

I AM WITH :

MY EXPECTATIONS :

WILDLIFE

SIGHTS

≫ — **ATTRACTIONS I VISITED** ⟶

○ Koyukuk River
○ Kobuk Wild River
○ Jhon river

○ Boreal Mountain
○ Kugururok River
○ Frigid Crags

○ -------------
○ -------------
○ -------------

VISITOR CENTER INFORMATION, NOTES, SKETCHES, etc.

My Best Moments

---

few words about
my visit

stamp here

RATING ☆☆☆☆☆

VISIT DATE
/ /20

← MISSOURI ≪

PARK N°

GATEWAY ARCH

Lodging

FEE(S) :

WEBSITE :
www.nps.gov/jeff

PHONE NUMBER :
314/655-1600

Weather

°F
( )

MOOD :

I AM WITH :

MY EXPECTATIONS :

WILDLIFE

SIGHTS

≫— ATTRACTIONS I VISITED ⟶

- ◯ retro elevator
- ◯ Old Cathedral
- ◯ Old Courthouse
- ◯ Busch Stadium
- ◯ City Garden
- ◯ Eads Bridge
- ◯ --------------
- ◯ --------------
- ◯ --------------

VISITOR CENTER INFORMATION, NOTES, SKETCHES, etc.

My Best Moments

few words about
my visit

stamp here

RATING ☆☆☆☆☆

VISIT DATE
/ /20

← ALASKA ≪

PARK N°

GLACIER BAY

Lodging

_____

FEE(S) :

WEBSITE :
www.nps.gov/glba

PHONE NUMBER :
907/697-2230

Weather

°F
(   )

MOOD : _____
_____

I AM WITH : _____
_____
_____

MY EXPECTATIONS : _____
_____
_____

WILDLIFE

SIGHTS

≫ — ATTRACTIONS I VISITED ⟶

○ Bartlett Cove
○ Sebree Island
○ Kayaking

○ Flight-seeing
○ Sunset at Halibut
○ Hiking

○ _____
○ _____
○ _____

VISITOR CENTER INFORMATION, NOTES, SKETCHES, etc.

My Best Moments

_____

_____

_____

— *few words about* —
—— *my visit* ——

----

stamp here

RATING ☆☆☆☆☆

← ALASKA ←≪

GLACIER

Lodging

_____

FEE(S) :

WEBSITE :
www.nps.gov/glac

PHONE NUMBER :
406/888-7800

Weather

°F
(   )

MOOD : _____

I AM WITH : _____

_____

_____

MY EXPECTATIONS : _____

_____

_____

WILDLIFE

SIGHTS

≫— ATTRACTIONS I VISITED ⟶

○ Grinnell Glacier   ○ Logan Pass   ○ _____
○ Lake McDonald   ○ St. Mary Lake   ○ _____
○ Avalanche Lake   ○ Trail of the Cedars ○ _____

VISITOR CENTER INFORMATION, NOTES, SKETCHES, etc.

── My Best Moments ──

_____

_____

_____

── *few words about* ──
── *my visit* ──

- -

- -

- -

stamp here

RATING ☆☆☆☆☆

VISIT DATE		PARK N°
/ /20	← ARIZONA ⪻	

GRAND CANYON

Lodging

_____

FEE(S) :

WEBSITE :	PHONE NUMBER :
www.nps.gov/grca	928/638-7888

Weather

°F
( )

MOOD : _____

I AM WITH : _____

MY EXPECTATIONS : _____

WILDLIFE

SIGHTS

≫— ATTRACTIONS I VISITED —→

○ Hiking a Trail   ○ Take a Scenic Drive   ○ _____
○ Ride a Mule   ○ Camping   ○ _____
○ Ride a Train   ○ Go on a Rafting Trip ○ _____

VISITOR CENTER INFORMATION, NOTES, SKETCHES, etc.

My Best Moments

few words about
my visit

stamp here

RATING ☆☆☆☆☆

VISIT DATE
_ _ / _ / 20 _ _

← —WYOMING— ≪

PARK N°
_ _ _ _ _ _ _

GRAND TETON

Lodging

_____

FEE(S) :

WEBSITE :
www.nps.gov/grte

PHONE NUMBER :
307/739-3399

Weather

°F
( )

MOOD : _____
_____

I AM WITH : _____
_____
_____

MY EXPECTATIONS : _____
_____
_____

WILDLIFE

SIGHTS

≫ — ATTRACTIONS I VISITED ⟶

○ Jenny Lake
○ Teton Park Road
○ Jackson Lake

○ Snake River Overlook
○ Schwabacher Landing
○ Moose Wilson Road

○ _____
○ _____
○ _____

VISITOR CENTER INFORMATION, NOTES, SKETCHES, etc.

My Best Moments

---

few words about my visit

----

stamp here

RATING ☆☆☆☆☆

VISIT DATE
/ /20

← NEVADA ←

PARK Nº

GREAT BASIN

Lodging

_____

FEE(S) :

WEBSITE :
www.nps.gov/grba

PHONE NUMBER :
775/234-7331

Weather

°F
( )

MOOD : _____
_____

I AM WITH : _____
_____
_____

MY EXPECTATIONS : _____
_____
_____

WILDLIFE

SIGHTS

≫ — ATTRACTIONS I VISITED ⟶

○ Lehman Caves
○ Wheeler Peak
○ Bristlecone Trails

○ Alpine Lakes Loop
○ Cuyahoga valley
○ Teresa Lake

○ _____
○ _____
○ _____

VISITOR CENTER INFORMATION, NOTES, SKETCHES, etc.

My Best Moments

---

few words about my visit

----

stamp here

RATING ☆☆☆☆☆

GREAT SAND DUNES

Lodging

_____

FEE(S) :

WEBSITE :
www.nps.gov/grsa

PHONE NUMBER :
719/378-6395

Weather

°F
( )

MOOD : _____
_____

I AM WITH : _____
_____
_____

MY EXPECTATIONS : _____
_____
_____

WILDLIFE

SIGHTS

≫ — **ATTRACTIONS I VISITED** ⟶

○ Go Sledding
○ See the Milky Way
○ Go for a Drive

○ Ranger Program
○ Sleep on the Sand
○ See a Waterfall

○ _____
○ _____
○ _____

VISITOR CENTER INFORMATION, NOTES, SKETCHES, etc.

My Best Moments

— few words about —
———— my visit ————

----

stamp here

RATING ☆☆☆☆☆

GREAT SMOKY MOUNTAINS

Lodging

FEE(S) :

WEBSITE :
www.nps.gov/grsm

PHONE NUMBER :
865/436-1200

Weather

°F
( )

MOOD : ____

I AM WITH : _____

MY EXPECTATIONS : _____

WILDLIFE

SIGHTS

≫── ATTRACTIONS I VISITED ⟶

- ◯ Foothills Parkway
- ◯ Clingmans Dome
- ◯ Cades Cove
- ◯ Laurel Falls
- ◯ Alum Cave Trail
- ◯ Newfound Gap Road
- ◯ --------------
- ◯ --------------
- ◯ --------------

VISITOR CENTER INFORMATION, NOTES, SKETCHES, etc.

My Best Moments

few words about my visit

----

stamp here

RATING ☆☆☆☆☆

GUADALUPE MOUNTAINS
Lodging

FEE(S) :

WEBSITE :
www.nps.gov/gumo

PHONE NUMBER :
915/828-3251

Weather

°F
( )

MOOD :

I AM WITH :

MY EXPECTATIONS :

WILDLIFE

SIGHTS

≫— ATTRACTIONS I VISITED ⟶

○ Hiking & camping
○ Dog Canyon
○ Horseback riding

○ Smith Spring
○ Stargazing
○ El Capitan

○ --------------
○ --------------
○ --------------

VISITOR CENTER INFORMATION, NOTES, SKETCHES, etc.

My Best Moments

_____

_____

_____

few words about
my visit

----

stamp here

RATING ☆☆☆☆☆

HALEAKALA

Lodging

_____

FEE(S) :

WEBSITE :
www.nps.gov/hale

PHONE NUMBER :
808/572-4400

Weather

°F
( )

MOOD : _____

I AM WITH : _____

MY EXPECTATIONS : _____

WILDLIFE

SIGHTS

≫— ATTRACTIONS I VISITED ⟶

○ Sunrise/Sunset   ○ Biking   ○ --------------
○ Hiking   ○ Horseback Riding   ○ --------------
○ Skywatching   ○ Ziplining   ○ --------------

VISITOR CENTER INFORMATION, NOTES, SKETCHES, etc.

——— My Best Moments ———

— few words about —
——— my visit ———

stamp here

RATING ☆ ☆ ☆ ☆ ☆

HAWAI'I VOLCANOES

Lodging

FEE(S) :

WEBSITE :
www.nps.gov/havo

PHONE NUMBER :
808/985-6000

Weather

°F
( )

MOOD : _____

I AM WITH : _____

MY EXPECTATIONS : _____

WILDLIFE

SIGHTS

≫— ATTRACTIONS I VISITED →

○ Hiking
○ Camping
○ Flora/Fauna

○ Kīlauea
○ Halema'uma'u
○ Mauna Ulu

○ _____
○ _____
○ _____

VISITOR CENTER INFORMATION, NOTES, SKETCHES, etc.

My Best Moments

_____

_____

_____

few words about
my visit

----

stamp here

RATING ☆☆☆☆☆

HOT SPRINGS

Lodging

_____

FEE(S) :

WEBSITE :
www.nps.gov/hosp

PHONE NUMBER :
501/620-6715

Weather

°F
( )

MOOD : _____
_____

I AM WITH : _____
_____
_____

MY EXPECTATIONS : _____
_____
_____

WILDLIFE

SIGHTS

≫ —— **ATTRACTIONS I VISITED** ⟶

○ Bathhouse Row   ○ Anthony Chapel   ○ _____
○ Fordyce Bathhouse ○ Lake Ouachita   ○ _____
○ Woodland Gardens   ○ Mountain Tower   ○ _____

VISITOR CENTER INFORMATION, NOTES, SKETCHES, etc.

My Best Moments

— few words about —
—— my visit ——

----

stamp here

RATING ☆☆☆☆☆

INDIANA DUNES

Lodging

- -

FEE(S) :

WEBSITE :
www.nps.gov/indu

PHONE NUMBER :
219/395-1882

Weather

°F
( )

MOOD : - - - - - -

I AM WITH : - - - - - - - - - - -

- - - - - - - - - - - - - - - - - -

- - - - - - - - - - - - - - - - - -

MY EXPECTATIONS : - - - - - - -

- - - - - - - - - - - - - - - - - - -

- - - - - - - - - - - - - - - - - - -

WILDLIFE

SIGHTS

≫ — ATTRACTIONS I VISITED ⟶

○ River Waterpark   ○ Majestic Star Casino   ○ - - - - - - - - - - - - -
○ Phare de Michigan   ○ Kemil Beach   ○ - - - - - - - - - - - - -
○ Mount Baldy   ○ Porter Beach   ○ - - - - - - - - - - - - -

VISITOR CENTER INFORMATION, NOTES, SKETCHES, etc.

My Best Moments

few words about
my visit

stamp here

RATING ☆☆☆☆☆

ISLE ROYALE

Lodging

_____

FEE(S) :

WEBSITE :
www.nps.gov/isro

PHONE NUMBER :
906/482-0984

Weather

°F
( )

MOOD : _____

I AM WITH : _____

_____

_____

MY EXPECTATIONS : _____

_____

_____

WILDLIFE

SIGHTS

≫ — **ATTRACTIONS I VISITED** ⟶

○ Rock Harbor
○ Scoville Point
○ Windigo Center

○ Suzy's Cave
○ Lookout Louise
○ Passage Island

○ _____
○ _____
○ _____

VISITOR CENTER INFORMATION, NOTES, SKETCHES, etc.

My Best Moments

_____

_____

_____

— *few words about —
—— my visit* ——

----

stamp here

RATING ☆☆☆☆☆

VISIT DATE
/ /20

← CALIFORNIA ≪

PARK N°

JOSHUA TREE

Lodging

FEE(S) :

WEBSITE :
www.nps.gov/jotr

PHONE NUMBER :
760/367-5500

Weather

°F
( )

MOOD : _____

I AM WITH : _____

MY EXPECTATIONS : _____

WILDLIFE

SIGHTS

≫ — ATTRACTIONS I VISITED →

○ Hidden Valley
○ Cholla Cactus
○ Keys View

○ Ryan Mountain
○ Arch Rock
○ Skull Rock

○ _____
○ _____
○ _____

VISITOR CENTER INFORMATION, NOTES, SKETCHES, etc.

My Best Moments

_____

_____

_____

—— *few words about* ——
—— *my visit* ——

----

stamp here

RATING ☆☆☆☆☆

VISIT DATE	← ALASKA ≪	PARK N°
_ _ / _ _ /20 _ _		_ _ _ _ _ _ _

KATMAI

Lodging

_____

FEE(S) :	WEBSITE : www.nps.gov/katm	PHONE NUMBER : 907/246-3305

Weather

°F
( )

MOOD : _____
_____

I AM WITH : _____	MY EXPECTATIONS : _____
_____	_____
_____	_____

WILDLIFE	SIGHTS

≫— **ATTRACTIONS I VISITED** ⟶

○ Brooks Falls   ○ Naknek Lake   ○ _____
○ Brooks River   ○ Savonoski Loop   ○ _____
○ Valley of Ten Thousand Smokes   ○ _____

VISITOR CENTER INFORMATION, NOTES, SKETCHES, etc.

My Best Moments

— *few words about* —
—— *my visit* ——

----

stamp here

RATING ☆☆☆☆☆

VISIT DATE	← ALASKA →	PARK N°
/ /20		

KENAI FJORDS

Lodging

_____

FEE(S) :	WEBSITE : www.nps.gov/kefj	PHONE NUMBER : 907/422-0500

Weather

°F
( )

MOOD : _____

I AM WITH : _____

_____

_____

MY EXPECTATIONS : _____

_____

_____

WILDLIFE

SIGHTS

≫— ATTRACTIONS I VISITED ⟶

- ◯ Glacier Exit
- ◯ Bear Glacier
- ◯ Glacier Aialik
- ◯ Aialik Bay
- ◯ Tonsina Point
- ◯ Lost Lake Trail
- ◯ _____
- ◯ _____
- ◯ _____

VISITOR CENTER INFORMATION, NOTES, SKETCHES, etc.

My Best Moments

_____

_____

_____

— few words about —
—— my visit ——

----

stamp here

RATING ☆☆☆☆☆

VISIT DATE
/ /20

← CALIFORNIA →

PARK N°

KINGS CANYON

Lodging

FEE(S) :

WEBSITE :
www.nps.gov/seki

PHONE NUMBER :
559/565-3341

Weather

°F
( )

MOOD : _____

I AM WITH : _____

MY EXPECTATIONS : _____

WILDLIFE

SIGHTS

≫— ATTRACTIONS I VISITED →

○ Giant Forest
○ Sherman Tree
○ Moro Rock Trail

○ Kings Canyon
○ Grant Grove
○ Congress Trail

○ --------------
○ --------------
○ --------------

VISITOR CENTER INFORMATION, NOTES, SKETCHES, etc.

My Best Moments

_____

_____

_____

few words about
my visit

----

stamp here

RATING ☆☆☆☆☆

KOBUK VALLEY

Lodging

FEE(S) :

WEBSITE :
www.nps.gov/chis

PHONE NUMBER :
(907) 442-3890

Weather

°F
( )

MOOD : ____

I AM WITH : _____

MY EXPECTATIONS : _____

WILDLIFE

SIGHTS

≫— ATTRACTIONS I VISITED —→

○ Hiking
○ Birding
○ Fishing

○ Camping
○ Aurora borealis
○ Observe wildlife

○ ----------
○ ----------
○ ----------

VISITOR CENTER INFORMATION, NOTES, SKETCHES, etc.

My Best Moments

_____

_____

_____

— *few words about* —
———— *my visit* ————

----

stamp here

RATING ☆☆☆☆☆

LAKE CLARK

Lodging

_____

FEE(S) :

WEBSITE :
www.nps.gov/lacl

PHONE NUMBER :
907/781-2218

Weather

°F
( )

MOOD : _____
_____

I AM WITH : _____
_____
_____

MY EXPECTATIONS : _____
_____
_____

WILDLIFE

SIGHTS

≫ — ATTRACTIONS I VISITED ⟶

○ Turquoise Lake
○ Chilikadrotna River
○ Mulchatna River

○ Turquoise Valley
○ Hiking
○ Camping

○ _____
○ _____
○ _____

VISITOR CENTER INFORMATION, NOTES, SKETCHES, etc.

My Best Moments

_____

_____

_____

— few words about —
— my visit —

----

stamp here

RATING ☆☆☆☆☆

LASSEN VOLCANIC

Lodging

_____

FEE(S) :

WEBSITE :
www.nps.gov/lavo

PHONE NUMBER :
530/595-4480

Weather

°F
( )

MOOD : _____

I AM WITH : _____

_____

_____

MY EXPECTATIONS : _____

_____

_____

WILDLIFE

SIGHTS

≫— ATTRACTIONS I VISITED ⟶

○ Mount Lassen
○ Manzanita Lake
○ Bumpass Hell

○ Sulphur Works
○ Cinder Cone
○ Kings Creek Falls

○ _____
○ _____
○ _____

VISITOR CENTER INFORMATION, NOTES, SKETCHES, etc.

── My Best Moments ──

_____

_____

_____

── few words about ──
── my visit ──

----

stamp here

RATING ☆☆☆☆☆

VISIT DATE
/ /20

← KENTUCKY →

PARK N°

MAMMOTH CAVE

Lodging

_____

FEE(S) :

WEBSITE :
www.nps.gov/maca

PHONE NUMBER :
270/758-2180

Weather

°F
(   )

MOOD : _____
_____

I AM WITH : _____
_____
_____

MY EXPECTATIONS : _____
_____
_____

WILDLIFE

SIGHTS

≫— ATTRACTIONS I VISITED ⟶

○ Crystal Onyx Cave   ○ Sand Cave   ○ _____
○ Diamond Caverns   ○ Green River   ○ _____
○ Gothic Avenue Tour ○ Dinosaur World   ○ _____

VISITOR CENTER INFORMATION, NOTES, SKETCHES, etc.

My Best Moments

— few words about —
—— my visit ——

stamp here

RATING ☆☆☆☆☆

MESA VERDE

Lodging

_____

FEE(S) :

WEBSITE :
www.nps.gov/meve

PHONE NUMBER :
970/529-4465

Weather

°F
( )

MOOD : _____

I AM WITH : _____

MY EXPECTATIONS : _____

WILDLIFE

SIGHTS

≫ — **ATTRACTIONS I VISITED** ⟶

○ Cliff Palace   ○ Spruce Tree House   ○ _____
○ Balcony House   ○ Hiking Trails   ○ _____
○ Long House   ○ Camping   ○ _____

VISITOR CENTER INFORMATION, NOTES, SKETCHES, etc.

My Best Moments

_____

_____

_____

— few words about —
——— my visit ———

----

stamp here

RATING ☆☆☆☆☆

← WASHINGTON ←

MOUNT RAINIER

Lodging

_____

FEE(S) :

WEBSITE :
www.nps.gov/mora

PHONE NUMBER :
360/569-2211

Weather

°F
( )

MOOD : _____
_____

I AM WITH : _____
_____
_____

MY EXPECTATIONS : _____
_____
_____

WILDLIFE

SIGHTS

≫── ATTRACTIONS I VISITED ⟶

○ Visit Paradise   ○ Silver Falls Trail   ○ ---------------
○ Observe Sunrise   ○ Skyline Trail   ○ ---------------
○ Fishing   ○ Camping   ○ ---------------

VISITOR CENTER INFORMATION, NOTES, SKETCHES, etc.

My Best Moments

few words about
my visit

----

stamp here

RATING ☆☆☆☆☆

NP of American Samoa

Lodging

_____

FEE(S) :

WEBSITE :	PHONE NUMBER :
www.nps.gov/npsa	684/633-7082

Weather

°F
(   )

MOOD : _____

I AM WITH : _____

MY EXPECTATIONS : _____

WILDLIFE

SIGHTS

≫— ATTRACTIONS I VISITED ⟶

○ Mount 'Alava   ○ Blunts Point Trail   ○ _____
○ Pago Pago Harbour   ○ Pola   ○ _____
○ Jean P Museum   ○ Matafao   ○ _____

VISITOR CENTER INFORMATION, NOTES, SKETCHES, etc.

My Best Moments

few words about my visit

stamp here

RATING ☆☆☆☆☆

← WASHINGTON →≪

NORTH CASCADES

Lodging

FEE(S) :

WEBSITE :
www.nps.gov/noca

PHONE NUMBER :
360/854-7200

Weather

°F
( )

MOOD : ____

I AM WITH : ____

MY EXPECTATIONS : ____

WILDLIFE

SIGHTS

≫— ATTRACTIONS I VISITED —→

○ Cascade Pass Trail   ○ Kayak   ○ ------------
○ Diablo Lake views   ○ Tulip Town   ○ ------------
○ Colonial Creek   ○ Camping   ○ ------------

VISITOR CENTER INFORMATION, NOTES, SKETCHES, etc.

My Best Moments

_____

_____

_____

few words about my visit

----

stamp here

RATING ☆☆☆☆☆

VISIT DATE
/ /20

← WASHINGTON ⋘

PARK N°

OLYMPIC

Lodging

FEE(S) :

WEBSITE :
www.nps.gov/olym

PHONE NUMBER :
360/565-3130

Weather

°F
( )

MOOD :

I AM WITH :

MY EXPECTATIONS :

WILDLIFE

SIGHTS

⋙— ATTRACTIONS I VISITED ⟶

○ Hoh Rain Forest
○ Hurricane Ridge
○ Ruby Beach

○ Staircase
○ Lake Crescent
○ Sol Duc Valley

○
○
○

VISITOR CENTER INFORMATION, NOTES, SKETCHES, etc.

My Best Moments

_____

_____

_____

— few words about —
— my visit —

----

stamp here

RATING ☆☆☆☆☆

PETRIFIED FOREST

Lodging

FEE(S) :

WEBSITE :
www.nps.gov/pefo

PHONE NUMBER :
928/524-6228

Weather

°F
( )

MOOD : _____

I AM WITH : _____

_____

_____

MY EXPECTATIONS : _____

_____

_____

WILDLIFE

SIGHTS

≫— ATTRACTIONS I VISITED —→

○ Painted Desert Inn   ○ Agate Bridge   ○ -------------
○ Blue Mesa   ○ Jasper Forest   ○ -------------
○ Crystal Forest   ○ Rainbow Forest   ○ -------------

VISITOR CENTER INFORMATION, NOTES, SKETCHES, etc.

My Best Moments

few words about
my visit

stamp here

RATING ☆☆☆☆☆

PINNACLES

Lodging

_____

FEE(S) :

WEBSITE :
www.nps.gov/pinn

PHONE NUMBER :
831/389-4485

Weather

°F
( )

MOOD : _____
_____

I AM WITH : _____
_____
_____

MY EXPECTATIONS : _____
_____
_____

WILDLIFE

SIGHTS

≫— ATTRACTIONS I VISITED →

○ Bear Gulch Cave   ○ Chalone Peak   ○ _____
○ High Peaks Trail   ○ North Chalone   ○ _____
○ Condor Gulch Trail   ○ Camping   ○ _____

VISITOR CENTER INFORMATION, NOTES, SKETCHES, etc.

My Best Moments

_____

_____

_____

— few words about —
— my visit —

----

stamp here

RATING ☆☆☆☆☆

VISIT DATE
/ /20

←—CALIFORNIA—≪

PARK N°

REDWOOD

Lodging

FEE(S) :

WEBSITE :
www.nps.gov/redw

PHONE NUMBER :
707/465-7335

Weather

°F
( )

MOOD :

I AM WITH :

MY EXPECTATIONS :

WILDLIFE

SIGHTS

≫—— ATTRACTIONS I VISITED ——→

○ Stout Memorial
○ Damnation Creek
○ Drive the Newton B

○ Roosevelt Elk
○ Gold Bluffs Beach
○ Camping

○ ------------
○ ------------
○ ------------

VISITOR CENTER INFORMATION, NOTES, SKETCHES, etc.

My Best Moments

_____

_____

_____

— few words about —
— my visit —

----

stamp here

RATING ☆☆☆☆☆

VISIT DATE		PARK N°
/ /20	← COLORADO ≪	

ROCKY MOUNTAIN

Lodging

_____

FEE(S) :

WEBSITE :	PHONE NUMBER :
www.nps.gov/romo	970/586-1206

Weather
☀ 🌤 ☁ ⛈ ❄

°F
(   )

MOOD : _____

_____

I AM WITH : _____

_____

_____

MY EXPECTATIONS : _____

_____

_____

WILDLIFE

SIGHTS

≫ — **ATTRACTIONS I VISITED** ⟶

○ Trail Ridge Road   ○ Emerald Lake   ○ _____
○ Downtown Estes   ○ Park Museum   ○ _____
○ Bear Lake   ○ Camping   ○ _____

VISITOR CENTER INFORMATION, NOTES, SKETCHES, etc.

My Best Moments

few words about
my visit

stamp here

RATING ☆☆☆☆☆

SAGUARO

Lodging

_____

FEE(S) :

WEBSITE :
www.nps.gov/sagu

PHONE NUMBER :
520/733-5153

Weather

°F
( )

MOOD : _____
_____

I AM WITH : _____
_____
_____

MY EXPECTATIONS : _____
_____
_____

WILDLIFE

SIGHTS

≫— ATTRACTIONS I VISITED ⟶

○ Desert Belle Cruises
○ Stellar Adventures
○ the Dolly Steamboat

○ Apache Trail Tours
○ Saguaro Lake
○ Kayaking

○ _____
○ _____
○ _____

VISITOR CENTER INFORMATION, NOTES, SKETCHES, etc.

My Best Moments

_____

_____

_____

— *few words about* —
—— *my visit* ——

- -

- -

- -

- -

stamp here

RATING ☆☆☆☆☆

SEQUOIA

Lodging

_____

FEE(S) :

WEBSITE :
www.nps.gov/seki

PHONE NUMBER :
559/565-3341

Weather

°F
( )

MOOD : _____

_____

I AM WITH : _____

_____

_____

MY EXPECTATIONS : _____

_____

_____

WILDLIFE

SIGHTS

≫— ATTRACTIONS I VISITED —→

○ Giant Forest
○ Kings Canyon scenic
○ General Sherman

○ Moro Rock
○ Crystal Cave
○ Tunnel Log

○ _____
○ _____
○ _____

VISITOR CENTER INFORMATION, NOTES, SKETCHES, etc.

My Best Moments

few words about
my visit

stamp here

RATING ☆☆☆☆☆

VISIT DATE	VIRGINIA	PARK N°
/ /20	← ←	

SHENANDOAH

Lodging

FEE(S) :

WEBSITE :
www.nps.gov/shen

PHONE NUMBER :
540/999-3500

Weather

°F
( )

MOOD : _____

I AM WITH : _____

MY EXPECTATIONS : _____

WILDLIFE

SIGHTS

≫— ATTRACTIONS I VISITED —→

○ Skyline Drive
○ Dark Hollow Falls
○ Hawksbill Mountain

○ Rose River Falls
○ Skyland
○ Camping

○ ---------------
○ ---------------
○ ---------------

VISITOR CENTER INFORMATION, NOTES, SKETCHES, etc.

——— My Best Moments ———

_____

_____

_____

— few words about —
——— my visit ———

----

stamp here

RATING ☆☆☆☆☆

THEODORE ROOSEVELT

Lodging

FEE(S) :

WEBSITE :
www.nps.gov/thro

PHONE NUMBER :
701/623-4466

Weather

°F
(   )

MOOD : _____

I AM WITH : _____

MY EXPECTATIONS : _____

WILDLIFE

SIGHTS

≫— ATTRACTIONS I VISITED ⟶

○ South Unit
○ Petrified Forest
○ Caprock-Coulee

○ Oxbow Overlook
○ Buckhorn Trail
○ Peaceful Valley

○ --------------
○ --------------
○ --------------

VISITOR CENTER INFORMATION, NOTES, SKETCHES, etc.

My Best Moments

few words about
my visit

stamp here

RATING ☆☆☆☆☆

VIRGIN ISLANDS

Lodging

FEE(S) :

WEBSITE :
www.nps.gov/viis

PHONE NUMBER :
340/776-2601

Weather

°F
( )

MOOD : _____

I AM WITH : _____

MY EXPECTATIONS : _____

WILDLIFE

SIGHTS

≫── ATTRACTIONS I VISITED ──→

- ◯ Honeymoon Beach
- ◯ Water Island
- ◯ Ram Head Trail
- ◯ Mountain Top
- ◯ Secret Harbour
- ◯ Coral Bay
- ◯ _____
- ◯ _____
- ◯ _____

VISITOR CENTER INFORMATION, NOTES, SKETCHES, etc.

My Best Moments

_____

_____

_____

— *few words about* —
— *my visit* —

----

stamp here

RATING ☆☆☆☆☆

VISIT DATE
/ /20

← — MINNESOTA — ≪

PARK Nº

VOYAGEURS

Lodging

FEE(S) :

WEBSITE :
www.nps.gov/voya

PHONE NUMBER :
218/283-6600

Weather

°F
( )

MOOD :

I AM WITH :

MY EXPECTATIONS :

WILDLIFE

SIGHTS

≫ — **ATTRACTIONS I VISITED** ⟶

○ Kettle Falls
○ Boat Tours
○ Camping

○ Canoeing
○ Cruising
○ Houseboating

○ ------------
○ ------------
○ ------------

VISITOR CENTER INFORMATION, NOTES, SKETCHES, etc.

My Best Moments

_____

_____

_____

— *few words about* —
—— *my visit* ——

----

stamp here

RATING ☆☆☆☆☆

WHITE SANDS

Lodging

_____

FEE(S) :

WEBSITE :
www.nps.gov/whsa

PHONE NUMBER :
575/479-6124

Weather

°F
( )

MOOD : _____
_____

I AM WITH : _____
_____
_____

MY EXPECTATIONS : _____
_____
_____

WILDLIFE

SIGHTS

≫— ATTRACTIONS I VISITED ⟶

- ○ Alameda Park Zoo
- ○ Peacock Playland
- ○ Shroud Exhibit
- ○ Toy Train Depot
- ○ Old Apple Barn
- ○ PistachioLand
- ○ _____
- ○ _____
- ○ _____

VISITOR CENTER INFORMATION, NOTES, SKETCHES, etc.

My Best Moments

_____

_____

_____

— *few words about* —
—— *my visit* ——

----

stamp here

RATING ☆☆☆☆☆

VISIT DATE	← — SOUTH DAKOTA — ≪	PARK Nº
_ / _ /20 _		_ _ _ _ _ _ _ _

WIND CAVE

Lodging

_ _

FEE(S) :	WEBSITE : www.nps.gov/wica	PHONE NUMBER : 605/745 4600

Weather	°F ( )	MOOD : _ _ _ _ _ _ _ _ _ _ _ _ _

I AM WITH : _ _ _ _ _ _ _ _ _ _

_ _ _ _ _ _ _ _ _ _ _ _ _ _ _

_ _ _ _ _ _ _ _ _ _ _ _ _ _ _

MY EXPECTATIONS : _ _ _ _ _ _

_ _ _ _ _ _ _ _ _ _ _ _ _ _ _

_ _ _ _ _ _ _ _ _ _ _ _ _ _ _

WILDLIFE

SIGHTS

≫ — **ATTRACTIONS I VISITED** ⟶

- ◯ Wind Cave Canyon
- ◯ Elk Mountain
- ◯ Rankin Ridge Trail
- ◯ Cold Brook
- ◯ Centennial Trail
- ◯ Boland Ridge
- ◯ _ _ _ _ _ _ _ _ _ _
- ◯ _ _ _ _ _ _ _ _ _ _
- ◯ _ _ _ _ _ _ _ _ _ _

VISITOR CENTER INFORMATION, NOTES, SKETCHES, etc.

My Best Moments

few words about
my visit

stamp here

RATING ☆☆☆☆☆

WRANGELL-ST. ELIAS
Lodging

_____

FEE(S) :

WEBSITE :
www.nps.gov/wrst

PHONE NUMBER :
907/822-5231

Weather

°F
( )

MOOD : _____

I AM WITH : _____

MY EXPECTATIONS : _____

WILDLIFE

SIGHTS

≫── ATTRACTIONS I VISITED ──→

○ Kennecott Mine
○ Nabesna Road
○ Mount Blackburn

○ Rambler Mine
○ Nugget Creek
○ Camping

○ _____
○ _____
○ _____

VISITOR CENTER INFORMATION, NOTES, SKETCHES, etc.

My Best Moments

---

few words about
my visit

stamp here

RATING ☆☆☆☆☆

Rames graduation

VISIT DATE	IDAHO MONTANA	PARK N°
/ /20	← WYOMING —«	

YELLOWSTONE

Lodging

Rames

FEE(S) :	WEBSITE : www.nps.gov/yell	PHONE NUMBER : 307/344-7381

Weather

°F (75)

MOOD : hung over

I AM WITH : mom, tm, mary, marty

MY EXPECTATIONS : more animals

WILDLIFE

overcrowded

SIGHTS

≫— ATTRACTIONS I VISITED —→

○ Lamar Valley　　○ Artist Point　　○ --------------
○ Prismatic Spring　○ Hayden Valley　○ --------------
⊘ Old Faithful　　○ Yellowstone river　○ --------------

VISITOR CENTER INFORMATION, NOTES, SKETCHES, etc.

My Best Moments

few words about
my visit

stamp here

RATING ☆☆☆☆☆

YOSEMITE

Lodging

_____

FEE(S) :

WEBSITE :
www.nps.gov/yose

PHONE NUMBER :
209/372-0200

Weather

°F
( )

MOOD : _____
_____

I AM WITH : _____
_____
_____

MY EXPECTATIONS : _____
_____
_____

WILDLIFE

SIGHTS

≫— **ATTRACTIONS I VISITED** —→

○ Yosemite Falls
○ Half Dome
○ El Capitan

○ Tunnel View
○ Glacier Point
○ Bridalveil Fall

○ _____
○ _____
○ _____

VISITOR CENTER INFORMATION, NOTES, SKETCHES, etc.

My Best Moments

few words about
my visit

stamp here

RATING ☆☆☆☆☆

← — UTAH — ≪

ZION

Lodging

_____

FEE(S) :

WEBSITE :	PHONE NUMBER :
www.nps.gov/zion	435/772-3256

Weather

°F
( )

MOOD : _____

I AM WITH : _____

MY EXPECTATIONS : _____

WILDLIFE

SIGHTS

≫— **ATTRACTIONS I VISITED** —→

○ The Narrows
○ Angel's Landing
○ Observation Point

○ Zion Shuttle
○ Emerald Pools
○ Riverside Walk

○ _____
○ _____
○ _____

VISITOR CENTER INFORMATION, NOTES, SKETCHES, etc.

My Best Moments

---

few words about my visit

stamp here

RATING ☆☆☆☆☆

YELLOWSTONE

≡ NATIONAL PARK ≡

REDWOOD

NATIONAL PARK

Made in the USA
Monee, IL
24 April 2021